I0484463

Table of Contents

What is Evernote?

Evernote is a revolutionary way to keep up with all the items on your to-do list. What makes the program so unique is its flexibility. You can install it on multiple devices. This means that you can say goodbye to the frustration that comes along with forgetting your to-do list.

Evernote can be used for business or personal purposes. Many people use it to organize every aspect of their lives. It's ridiculously easy to use and can be customized to fit the needs of the user. Evernote has both a free and a paid version which we will talk about in more detail a little later in the book.

One of the coolest things about Evernote is that you can do more than just store multiple lists. It can also hold photos, recipes, and other important items. In this book, we will discuss the basic and advanced features of Evernote and how they can be used to increase your productivity and organize your life. When you are more productive and organized, reaching your goals become easier. At the end of this book, we will tell you about one of the most powerful ways in which you can make the most of Evernote.

Why Should I Use Evernote?

You should use Evernote because of its incredibly easy flexibility. It gives you the opportunity to organize your entire life. You could use it to save recipes that you find on websites and then create a portable grocery list. You could use it to remind you of important tasks. You could use it to manage your daily to-do list. There are a lot of add-ons that are available for you to enhance Evernote. We discuss some of these toward the end of the book. However, that's not an all inclusive list. You can find add-ons for Evernote for just about anything. We do discuss one particular website later that lists more than 9000 options that you can use for Evernote.

Many people use Evernote to manage their personal and business lives. This is one of the few systems available that enables a user to seamlessly integrate their lists. That means you won't have to use separate programs. You can even forward emails into Evernote. This saves you time. We will talk more about the email feature later in this ebook.

You can choose to start with a free account. Working with a free Evernote account can help you decide if a paid account is right for you. You get a lot of great features with a free account. That will give you an excellent idea on whether Evernote will help you organize your life. Many of the advanced features will work with the free account.

Evernote is great for people who have a ton of ideas. So, if you are a highly creative person then Evernote is definitely for you. It can also help just about everyone improve their daily organization. It allows you to begin your personal journey to a paperless life. You might not ever go totally paperless, but it's a good start.

Evernote can be used for more than just keeping lists of any sort. Here are some other ways that you can use it.

- You can use Evernote as a journal. You can even protect your information by encryption.

- You can create a note that acts as a go-between for you and another person. This can serve as a way to stay in communication or keep dual notes on a particular situation. You'll never have to worry about an email going into spam again.
- Keep clothing sizes and other pertinent gift information on hand. If you do the shopping for your family or if you have a lot of gifts that you buy, you can keep that information available for easy access.
- Use Evernote as a digital contact management system. You can use an add-on or even just use a spreadsheet.
- Send voice memos to yourself. Evernote has a way that allows you to record audio files. This is an excellent way to save your last minute ideas.

There are entire websites that are devoted to unique ways that you can use Evernote in your life.

Free or Premium? Pros and Cons

You have two choices when it comes to using Evernote. You can use the free version or you can opt to pay an extremely low fee and get the premium version. The free version of Evernote is still quite functional. In fact, it's good enough for most people to get started.

A free account, however, does have several limitations. You can only upload 60 MB per month. You can only access your notebooks while you are connected to the Internet. While people can see your notebooks, they cannot edit them. So, if you work in a team environment then Evernote free may not be the best choice for you. Also, your notes cannot be any larger than 25 MB. However, you can still attach files such as Powerpoints and PDFs as long as you don't go over your maximum upload amount. You can only have 100 notebooks. You technically get unlimited storage, but again be mindful of the monthly upload limit. You can only send 50 messages per day to your customized Evernote email address. As you can see, there are limitations. However, you can use the main features of Evernote for free to determine if it's a good fit for your life.

Evernote premium accounts are really inexpensive. For individual users, it is around $5 per month. They also offer business plans. Generally, the more people that are part of your business, the cheaper your monthly rate would be. Not only do the limitations of the free account disappear, but you get some really cool extra features.

- Your monthly upload limit is increased to 1 gig. You still get unlimited storage space.
- Your notes can be as large as 100 MG. You're probably thinking that's a lot of text (even if your file were only 25MB). Keep in mind that your note can include more than text. It can include photos, audio, or other things.
- You can have more notebooks. A premium account allows you to set up 250 notebooks.
- You can send up to 200 emails to your Evernote account per day.
- You can work with other people through a premium account. People can view and edit your notes. This is great for collaboration.
- Premium members get faster support than free members.

- You can access your notebooks even if you're not connected to the Internet. If you travel for business, then you know how important it is to be able to access your work files while you're on the go.
- You can protect your files with a passcode.
- If you read a lot of PDF files, a premium Evernote account enables you to add annotations to your PDFs.
- You have an amazing number of add-ons available to customize your experience.

Installation

Installing Evernote is quick and easy even for those who don't have a lot of experience using personal productivity apps. First, you need to determine on what devices you want to install it. You can install it to your computer or your smart device. For our purposes, a smart device will include a smart phone or a tablet.

1. You must download the Evernote program or app. Visit the Evernote website to find the download link for your computer. Visit the app store for your smart device. Evernote is available for Apple and Android products. An automatic download will start when you visit the download page of the website.
2. Install the program. If you are on your computer, go to the folder where your downloads are stored. Double click the Evernote installation file. If you are installing it on your smart device, it will normally automatically install itself after you download it. Remember to pay attention to the license agreement. Follow the steps presented in the computer installation.

3. Make sure and install the program on all the devices that you wish to use to access your account.
4. Register for an Evernote account. Remember, you can register for a free account. If you are on your computer, you can look at the right side of the open program. You will see an option in the sidebar that says "New to Evernote." You can fill out the fields to register. If you have an account, click "Already have an account" to log in. This is located in the bottom right hand corner.

Familiarizing Yourself with the App

It's important that you get to know Evernote. First, let's go over where you can find everything. In the next section, we will discuss the basic things you should know so that you can get started with your account. It's important to note that if you use Evernote on a Mac that your layout may be a little different than Windows. It's not so different that you won't be able to find your way around.

Top Area

When you look at the top of Evernote, you will see several things. You'll see a search bar. Searching in Evernote is ridiculously easy. Your notes are searchable. The tags that you apply are searchable. In instances where you utilize the OCR feature for pictures, then those become searchable as well.

Directly to the right of the search, you see a plus sign. It says New Note. If you click this, then you will be able to start a brand new note. It really can't get much easier than that when it comes to starting a new note!

Sidebar

On the left of your screen, you will see the sidebar. Now, if you haven't made a few notebooks, notes, and tags then you may not see much over there. Here are a few things that you should know about the sidebar. Eventually, you will have Stacks. Those are notebooks that are related to each other. You will see Notebooks. A notebook is a collection of notes.

Notes are, of course, the writings that you put into Evernote to be saved. Remember that your notes are not relegated to text only. You can add pictures, audio files, and even computer files (like a PDF or a Powerpoint).

Note Area

You can see your notes in two spots. Next to the Sidebar, you will see a window that says All Notes. It will give you a preview of whatever note that you want to see. When you click on a note, it will appear a little bit to the right in an area that will allow you to edit your note.

At the top of the note area, you will see a spot to put a title. You don't need to be creative about this (but you can if you want). This is the spot where you can, essentially, put in a short description of what your note covers. You can assign it to a particular notebook and also assign tags.

The area in which you draft your note looks a little bit like a word processor. You'll see an area that allows you to format your font or other things in your note. Then, you'll see the area where you type, Again, it doesn't just have to be text. You can embed pictures. You can put in audio files. Just remember what we said earlier about your monthly upload limitation.

The Basics

In this section, we are going to talk about the basics of using Evernote. The basics are the same regardless of whether you use a free or premium account. Make sure that you pay attention to this section. You really need a firm grip of the basic features in order to make Evernote work well for you. Also, knowing how to use the basics will help you master the more advanced features that we will discuss later.

Creating Notes

First, we are going to take a more detailed look at creating notes. Notes are the building block of Evernote. Your notes are organized into Notebooks. Your Notebooks can be organized into Stacks. So, it's important that you know exactly what a note is and what you can do with it.

Let's look at some of the things that you can add to a note.

- Audio records – this can be a voicemail that was emailed to you, a podcast, or any other audio recording that you have. You probably have audio recording capability on your smart phone. So, if you're an audible learner, you can record yourself and then add it to a note to access at a later time.
- Manuals – this is particularly helpful if you plan to use Evernote for business purposes.
- PDF files – you can even annotate your PDF files.
- Pictures – the cool thing about pictures (and we will talk about pictures in more detail later) is that you can make them searchable by utilizing Evernote's OCR capability.

- Web pages – this is great for just about any personal or business purpose. It keeps vital information at the tip of your fingers.
- Personal writing – you don't have to just save things from the Internet or files that people send you. You can simply type up a note. It can be business, personal, or something creative.
- Documents – you can add documents to your notes regardless of if you have a free or premium account. However, if you have a premium account then you can collaborate with other people and it can be saved right there to Evernote.

You can add mixed media to your notes. It doesn't have to be a note with just one audio recording. Your note can also have a PDF file or even a document. It could also have something that you added in text format. The only real limitation for a note is the size. Free accounts get less monthly upload space than a premium account. However, you should also know that you're probably not going to make a single note that would take up all of your monthly upload space... unless you're just going out of your way to do that.

When you are looking at an individual note, you'll notice a few things that you can do. You'll see the plus sign that we talked about a little earlier. We use this button if we want to create a new note. Below that, you'll see an area where you can choose your Notebook. It looks like a scroll box. Right next to the notebook choice box, you'll see an area to add your tags. Tags are optional. You can have one tag or as many tags as you would like.

You'll see a bar on the note that allows you to edit your font and other features of your note. This is commonly referred to as an editor's toolbar. There are a lot of things that you can do. You can, of course, format your text. You can also create simple tables and add checkboxes to create a to-do list.

On the right side of the screen, you will see an option that says Info. With it, you can work with multiple people and perform other functions. However, this feature is only available for those with premium accounts.

Beneath share and info, you will see something that resembles a tiny checkbox. This button allows you to set up a reminder. We will go through the functions of this feature in more detail a little later. It was brought up here because it is part of the note screen.

Near the reminder feature, you'll see a trash can. That is, of course, what you would press should you decide to delete your note. There's really no need to delete notes unless you just really don't like the clutter of notes that you no longer need. After all, you can store up to 100,000 notes in Evernote.

Beneath the editor's toolbar, you will see the area where you title your note. As discussed earlier, you do not have to give it a long or creative title. It can simply be something that will remind you of what the note contains. Then, of course, you have the body of the note. We already discussed the types of things that you can put into the body of the note. You can even copy and paste information that you find online or from an email (or other computer document) directly into a note.

You can edit and update your note from any of your platforms. If you make a note on your computer and if you've synched Evernote to all your devices, then you could edit it from your smart phone and save it. This automatically updates the file.

This is why Evernote is a great tool for collaborative work. It's also great for people on the go.

Notebook Mastery

The Notebooks are another key organizational method of Evernote. Your notes are placed into Notebooks that you create. If you have hundreds or even thousands of notes, then you'd have a hard time finding just the right note. Placing your notes into specific Notebooks can help minimize the frustration of finding what you need. In short, Notebooks keep your notes organized.

You should know that each note can only be included in one Notebook. The way to solve this in the instance that you have a note that you want to appear in multiple places is to utilize the tags that we discussed earlier.

You can arrange your Notebooks in the way that best suits you. If you look online, you will find lots of tips and methods on how people believe Notebooks are best managed and organized. You could start by creating Notebooks for each major area of your life. This could be as simple as making a Notebook for home and one for Business.

There are five steps to Notebook Mastery. The good news is that the steps are quite simple.

1. Create your default Notebook. This is your Notebook that is just a standard Notebook without much in the way of organization. If you don't use tags or any sort of filtering in advance, Evernote will put notes into your default Notebook. All of your untagged Notes or

unassigned notes will go directly into this Notebook. Give it a name that you will easily remember. You don't want to accidently misplace an important note that you didn't have time to tag. . Creating a Notebook is easy. Just right click or tap on Notebooks on the left side of your screen. Then, choose 'Create Notebook.'

2. Use specific Notebooks. The problem with only using a single Notebook is that it will quickly get cluttered. Make some Notebooks that are specific. You can edit these in the future to reflect any changes to your life.

3. Synchronize your Notebooks. If you need to access any or all of your Notebooks from other devices, then you need to make sure that you synch them. You have the option of making a Notebook something that can only be accessed from that specific device. This type of Notebook will be called a Local Notebook.

4. Pick your sharing options for your Notebooks. You can give other people access to your Notebooks. With a free account, they can only view your Notebooks. With a premium account, you can choose to let other people edit your Notebooks. Generally, when a Notebook is shared it cannot be edited.

5. Make sure that your Notebooks are organized. You will use labels to organize your Notebooks. You could use inbox, action, ideas, and random. Those are very basic labels that can get you started with organizing.

Using Stacks to Organize Notebooks

Using Stacks is Evernote's way of organizing your Notebooks. Essentially, these are Notebooks that meet some sort of common criteria. Evernote describes Stacks as "digital dividers for your cloud-based filing system." You are able to take related Notebooks and group them. If you loved travel, then you could make a Stack called "Travel" and put all of your Notebooks about places you want to travel to inside of this Stack.

Creating a Stack is really easy. There are two ways that you can do it. The first way involves just dragging and dropping related Notebooks on top of each other. Then, add a title to your new Stack. The second method is to click on a Notebook that is not already part of a Stack. Then you can move it by using the "Add to stack" option. You can move it to an existing Stack or you can create a new Stack.

Shortcuts

You can also merge your notes. However, this is something that you should really consider before you jump the gun and do it. Merging is easy. You choose the notes that you want to merge and use Control and Click on a PC. You'll get a thumbnail view of the combined notes. You'll get options to add tags, merge, and move to a different notebook. Then, just click Merge. This will turn those notes into a single note.

Adding photos to your notes is easy. You can do it from any of your devices. This is another reason why people love Evernote. Let's say that you take a great picture with your smart phone. Let's say that you have photo editing software on your computer. You don't have to plug your smart phone into your computer. You can simply put the photo in a note. Then, you can access it from your computer. Simply create a new note or open an existing note. You can either drag the image into the note or use the paperclip from your computer. On an Apple smart device, you use the paperclip or the camera icon. Then, go into your photos. For Android devices, use the camera icon for a new picture or press the plus icon and pick attachment if you want to add an existing picture to a note.

Adding audio is simple. You open an existing note or start a new note. Then, you can click the microphone or click the plus icon if you already have something recorded. Yes, that's right. Evernote can record the audio for you using the microphone.

Here are some other great shortcuts that will make using Evernote a productive and easy experience.

- You should try using the checklists feature for your projects. You can simply check off your tasks as you complete them.
- Set up alarm emails. This feature will send you an email to remind you.
- Try out note encryption. You can easily protect sensitive or personal information.

Reminders

Reminders are great. You have a couple of different options for Evernote. You can use the alarm emails that we discussed in Shortcuts. You can also use the reminders option located in your note. There are presets available to define your clicks.

For one click, you can set something for tomorrow or one week. You can also customize it with any date that you want even if it's a year out or more.

Sharing

On the right side of the screen (near the tags, but on the other side of the screen) you will see an option to share your note. Sharing is extremely helpful in many instances. You could share your note via email, social media, or any third party platform that supports Evernote.

Annotation

If you work with others, you might find that annotating your PDFs is a regular occurrence. You can do that in Evernote. You can add words, lines, and other things to draw attention to specific parts of the PDF. Premium users receive a summary feature for their annotations. You should know that annotation is not available for Windows based computers at the time this book is written. Using a Mac, you press Control and click on a PDF and pick Annotate this PDF. Using an Apple smart device, just open the PDF and select the option to annotate. For Android smart device users, follow the direction for Apple smart devices.

With the annotation tool, you can do more than just what we've already discussed or what you may think of as typical annotation methods. You can also pixelate images or information. If you make a mistake, it's no problem. Just pick Edit and clear your annotations.

Syncing

You can sync your account to whatever devices that you have Evernote running on. If you have it on your computer, you can sync it to your smart phone. You just go to Tools – Options – Sync. This is one of the reasons why Evernote is so popular. You can take your lists with you practically anywhere you go.

Tags

We talked a little bit about tags. Tags are optional labels that you can apply to a note. You can use as few or as many as you would like. Tags make searching for your notes easier. This is particularly handy if you work with a large amount of notes or notebooks. It's also great if you do work on collaborative projects. It makes notes easier to find for your colleagues.

Tags are an organizational system to find your information. They are different than Notebooks. You can use tags, Notebooks, or both. Tags provide an additional way to find information than searching through a large Notebook or even a Stack.

Tagging is easy. There are two ways to do it. First, you can do it when you create a new note. Depending on the device, you would click "Click to add tag" or you'd look under Note Details. The second way to add tags is available to those who use Evernote from an computer instead of a smart device. On the left side of your computer screen you will see a list of tags. You can simply click the down arrow to add a new tag or you can apply tags that you've already create.

For tags to work well for you, you should find a particular way that you tag things and stick to it. For instance, if you have a Notebook for Christmas, you would want to pick and stick with either Christmas or Xmas. If you had Christmas and Xmas, then you might have to do twice the searching to find whatever you were looking for to begin with.

Using plural words for tags is very efficient. The reasoning is simple. If you used "cats" as your tag, you could even just search on the word "cat" and get results. As you see, this makes it easier to find. Using a singular version of a word and then searching on the plural version will often result in a return of zero results.

If you make tags that are for people, use their first name and their last initial as the tag. This makes it easier to find things if you know more than one person with the same name.

Use who, what, where, when, and why if you are not sure how to tag your notes. You can start with broad subjects (like recipes) and then move on to narrow subjects (like grilled chicken).

Try not to use tags that contain more than one word. This can make it hard to find exactly the note that you are looking for. This is particularly true if you planned to use a year in the tag name. Finding chicken recipes is much easier than finding 2014 chicken recipes. Besides, what if you didn't save the particular recipe in 2014? Instead, you could use "chicken," "recipes," and "year" all as tags.

Making Evernote Search Work for You

Searching with Evernote is ridiculously easy. The search feature is also quite powerful. The best part about the search feature is that you really don't need any sort of special rules or formulas to conduct a search. You just type in what you are trying to find. If you are searching for documents, pictures, or other uploads that you put information about Belize in, then you could just type in Belize. It would bring back all pictures, documents, notes, notebooks, and anything else tagged with the word Belize.

There are special search techniques that you can use. If you use words like "created" or "updated" followed by a colon and a YYYYMMDD, you can find specific info that you wanted that you couldn't remember. You can also restrict your search to certain fields.

The search feature does more than just search on tags. If you heard a certain term at a meeting and you made a note, then you can just search on the term. Evernote pulls words from tags, metadata, content, and from OCR. Here are a few more search tips for those who want to know more about refining their search.

- Using a start at the end of a word will give you results for anything that includes the word or comes after the word in a block of text.
- Your search doesn't have to be exact. "Eggs and bacon" will still come up when the title or text you were looking for said "bacon and eggs."
- Capitalization doesn't matter.
- You can save your searches.

- You can search specific Notebooks. notebook: [Notebook name] search term.
- You can search by tags only. Tag: [Tag name]
- You can search by title. intitle: [search terms].

Enhance Pictures with OCR

OCR is an interesting and unique feature of Evernote. Although we are focusing on pictures, you can also use the OCR feature on any hand written notes that you upload into the program.

OCR stands for optical character recognition. In layman's terms, it essentially means that your computer can read the words in photos. It recognizes those words as text. Those words are then searchable.

Advanced Evernote Use

Now that you know all the basics of Evernote, we are going to talk about some of the more advanced features. There are a lot of amazing things that Evernote can do to make your entire life easier. This is true even if you have a free account.

Importing Email

Importing email is a great productivity tool and time saver. It's a great way to save important emails or even create a list of items that you need to do. While it's probably not recommended that you send every email to Evernote, you should definitely consider sending all of your important ones. Just be mindful of your daily limit (which is dependent upon the type of account that you have). Below, we've outlined the steps you need to take to set up your email-to-Evernote.

1. Find out your unique Evernote email. This is important. Everyone that signs up for Evernote is assigned one. No two are exactly the same. It does look like an email address, but it is generally more than just your name. To find this, open Evernote. Then, go to Tools and then Account Info. You will see a link that says "email note to." Copy that link.
2. Add the Evernote email address to your email contact list. You can call the contact Evernote or something that you will recognize. Paste in the Evernote email address that you copied in Step 1. You can either forward emails to that address or follow a more advanced strategy that we will soon discuss.
3. Make sure that you have a default Notebook set up. We talked about the benefits of a default Notebook earlier

in this book. This is important because most of the time you might not take the time to tag your emails that you are forwarding to Evernote. Your default Notebook holds all of your unfiltered notes. Emails will most often count as an unfiltered note.

4. Know how to use tags. If you know how to use tags, then your email won't be dropped into your default Notebook. You can set it up to go somewhere else in Evernote. It's easy, but it can take a few tries to learn. First, get ready to send something to the Evernote email address. In the subject line, give it a title that describes the content of the email. After the title, use @Notebook Name. Then, your email will be directed to a specific Notebook. If you had a Travel Notebook, you would use @Travel. After the destination you can add specific tags by first using a hashtag. Yes, just like you see on social media.

Automate Your Email Delivery

You can automate your email to make it go directly to Evernote. This is not ideal if you receive a lot of email every day. However, it is a good way to filter your email. There is a specific process involved to do this. Please keep in mind that this process can vary depending upon your current email client. This walk through for email delivery automation is geared toward Outlook since that's the client that most people use at home. If you use Gmail or another popular email provider, there are walk through tutorials available online for you to consult. The best way to do this is to search on the email client and the term email forwarding. You could even search on how to forward email to Evernote from email client.

In Outlook, click the gear symbol. Then, click Options and then Email Forwarding. You will see an option that says "Forward your email to another email account." Click that option and put in the Evernote email address. Click save.

Scan Documents with CamScanner

Remember that earlier when we talked about OCR and pictures that we briefly mentioned that you could even use OCR on hand written documents. Well, to get those documents into Evernote, they must first be scanned. Most scanners work really well with Evernote. In this section, we will discuss using the CamScanner app. You're probably wondering why you would want to use an app. Well, it simplifies things for you. You won't have to go in and mess with a lot of scanner and Evernote options in order to scan in your hand written documents or things that you have around that you want backed up to Evernote.

CamScanner is great because it utilizes your smart phone camera. You just download the app, turn it on, and pass it over the document using a smooth motion. It works well with Evernote and it can incorporate OCR to make finding your files easier.

IFTTT Recipes

IFTTT is an acronym that stands for If this, then that. There is a website and an app available. Essentially, it's like if A happens, then B will happen after that. Hence the name of the app and website being IFTTT; you probably learned the principle while you were still in school.

You should know IFTTT Recipes doesn't work in every browser. It does work really well with Firefox. Recipes isn't what you think. This isn't about cooking. They use the word to discuss their favorite programs and apps. They list almost 9000 apps for Evernote.

Check it out and find the ones that will best increase your organization and productivity. You'll find ways to organize your receipts, back up your tweets, download Instagram photos, connect Google Talk, send your RSS feed to Evernote, and more. IFTTT has a search bar to help you find things that you might want to use. They also offer a ton of ideas that you can use to make Evernote benefit you.

Importing Folders

If you have documents that you're worried about losing, then you can import them into Evernote. You can set up your computer to pay attention to one specific folder and copy anything you put inside of it to Evernote. Once it is in Evernote, you can tag things and give those things better descriptions.

Here's how to import your folders from a Windows based computer:

1. Create your folder or choose an existing folder that you want to import to Evernote. Remember, this information will be stored on a cloud server. Make sure that you are comfortable with that. If your file is sensitive and requires a password, you might want to think about whether or not you really want to back it up to a cloud

server. Make sure that your folder has an easy to remember name such as Evernote Backup.

2. In Evernote, choose Tools. Then, choose Import Folders and click Add.

3. Pick any folder that you want to import. Make sure that you also choose any subfolders that are in that particular folder. If you don't take this step, then those folders will not be backed up to Evernote.

4. If you need to delete a file that you've added to Evernote, just click the dropdown menu and pick Delete.

Using the import feature is a great tool if you travel a lot. You won't have to worry about something happening that would make it impossible to access your files.

Encryption

You can encrypt your files with Evernote. This is particularly helpful if you have imported your files from your computer. You can encrypt online documentation such as receipts. Encrypting your files is also an added layer of protection against data breeches. The following method can be used to encrypt existing Evernote files:

To encrypt part of an existing note, start by highlighting the text. Then, right click to bring up the menu. Select the option that says "Encrypt Selected Text." You will be prompted to enter a password and confirm it. Evernote will not store this password for you. Make sure that you choose a password that you can remember.

You will not be able to read the encrypted text without putting in the new password. You will have an option to permanently unencrypt your file or selected text.

Evernote Add-Ons

Evernote has a lot of add-ons that you can install in order to customize your experience. They will make using Evernote more personal and maybe even a little more fun.

Evernote Web Clipper

Evernote Web Clipper is one of the most popular add-ons. It's an extension that you add to a web browser. You can import text, data, pictures, and files into Evernote while you are surfing the web. You don't have to save the entire article, either. You can choose just part of the article.

Evernote Clearly

Evernote Clearly is another great add-on. The premise is simple. You add it to your favorite browser much like you do for Web Clipper. You can save blog posts, articles, or other things that you find on the web and read it later without the advertisements. You can customize it with a theme or even build your own theme.

Evernote Hello

Evernote Hello will help you remember the people that you meet. You can save people in alphabetical order by name. Then, you can add a picture and information such as where and when you met them. This is a great Evernote tool for those who meet a lot of new people on a regular basis. It's also great if you attend a lot of meetings or if you are in the sales profession. You could use it to keep up with your sales prospects. You can also add people that you meet online!

Skitch

This is another free add-on. You can use it to turn your images such as screenshots or photos into something that you can mar up. So, you could highlight words, add arrows to show someone something important, crop, and you can even resize your pictures. It's a great add-on for collaboration. After you use Skitch and do what you want to your image, then you can save it and send it to Evernote just by the push of a button. You can also share your edited images to your social media accounts. You can also save your images in different formats or even turn it into a PDF file.

Yummy!

Evernote Yummy is now known as Evernote Food. You can do a lot with this add-on. It's great for foodies or even just people who love recipes. You can share recipes, find great ideas, and even read restaurant reviews. You can even save your favorite restaurants into the app. This app is available in the Apple app store for free.

Peek

Peek is a great study tool. It shows you the question and then reveals the answer to show you if you are right. This is really cool if you have a cover for your iPad. It will show you the answer when you lift the cover. If you use Evernote on a device that doesn't have a cover, you can choose to use a virtual cover. You can even access content that was created by professionals.

FileThis Fetch

This add-on can grab your online statements, bills, or other documents from places like Amazon. You won't have to log in manually. It provides a single place within Evernote to store all of your billing information. Please be careful if you decide to use this add-on. You really want to make sure that your information is totally secure.

The Secret Weapon to Get Things Done

Getting things done (GTD) is a productivity methodology that can be used with Evernote. It's particularly powerful when it is combined with techniques found in *The Secret Weapon Manifesto*. In this final section, we will discuss how you can use GTD productivity and *The Secret Weapon Manifesto* to complete more tasks and meet your goals using Evernote. Combining the two techniques in Evernote gives users a powerful way to get things done. To use both of these productivity methods and get the maximum results, you must have Evernote installed on all of your devices. We also recommend that you read both the book *Getting Things Done* by David Allen and *The Secret Weapon Manifesto* introduction page.

We will discuss *The Secret Weapon Manifesto* in more detail a little later in this section. First, let's discuss GTD methodology. Then, we will discuss a little about *The Secret Weapon Manifesto* and why the two methods combined are very powerful for Evernote users.

The book *Getting Things Done* by David Allen is a national best seller. It is where the GTD methodology is fully explained and developed. It acts as a productivity method that, on its face, is very simple. On its own, it doesn't require any sort of program or tool. We just happen to think it works really well with Evernote. The idea behind the book and the method is to take your never ending to-do list and get everything on it as organized as possible. The more organized that your tasks are in a way that you can see, then the easier they will be to complete. You use this method to prioritize your list by importance and by the amount of time that it will take to complete each item. It also discusses taking larger projects and breaking them down into manageable steps that you can complete faster. Those are the basic steps for using GTD. The book goes into detail about how you can use it for all of your daily tasks.

There are five core pillars that support GTD and how it works.

1. You should capture everything…and the author means everything: your ideas, your tasks. Essentially, you should capture anything that you need to do at any point in time. It doesn't matter if it is something you do every day or something that you won't do until next month.
2. Clarify what you need to accomplish. This is the act of breaking down your tasks into actionable steps. Think of it this way: you don't just go into the kitchen and decide that you want homemade pizza. You have to follow a recipe and take the steps to make the pizza.
3. Organize your actionable items by category and by priority. We talk more about how you can do this when we discuss *The Secret Weapon Manifesto.*
4. Reflect on your list. The goal is to find anything that is too vague and clarify it. This will also allow you to see where you are making progress.
5. Engage your list and get started. You want to start with the items that you prioritized as most important.

The Secret Weapon Manifesto is available online. It combines the power of email, Evernote, and GTD to give you the most effective and efficient way to use Evernote. Many of us use our email inboxes as a place to keep a virtual to-do list. We might email ideas to ourselves. We may keep the things that we need to do or emails that we need to respond to. Before we know it, our inbox becomes out of control. Some people simply file email bankruptcy by deleting everything and vowing to start over.

The Secret Weapon Manifesto capitalizes on GTD and basically gives what it calls a "no task left behind" system of to-do list organization. The idea is that when we are able to control our lists in a focused manner, we are better able to focus on what needs to be done. The ability to sync Evernote on multiple devices is key to using this system for maximum results. This allows you the ability to access your list no matter where you happen to be at any given moment.

Using *The Secret Weapon Manifesto* relies heavily on tags and how you have your notebooks set up. For this productivity method, you should have three basic notebooks: cabinet (to hold the items that you don't need to worry about any time soon), action pending (a list that holds everything from going to the grocery store to your largest project), and completed. There are several header tags that you should use if you are going to implement this system:

- What
- When
- Where
- Who
- Active
- Inactive
- Daily
- 1 – Now
- 2 – Next
- 3 – Soon
- 4 – Later

- 5 – Some day
- 6 – Waiting
- Home
- Work
- Town
- Read / review

You can also set up tags using the first or last names of people that you have appointments with or things that you need to complete for them. You can always add or delete additional tags as you see fit.

Now, you have to organize your tags. Under 'What,' you should drag your Active, Inactive, and Read / review items. Those will be your nested tags. Under 'When,' drag your Daily tag and the items listed above as 1-6 as your nested tags. Under 'Who,' drag the tags that you named after people. Under 'Where,' drag the tags of Home, Work, and Town. This nesting is important because it keeps your to-do list thoroughly organized. Remember that according to GTD, the more organized we can make our list that the better we can tackle it. Finally, you will add your to-do list items into the right tags. Each item will be its own note. Start with emptying your email inbox. You will only move emails to Evernote if you need to complete a task involved in the email. It could be as simple as calling someone back. Delete or archive the emails that you don't need. You can move your emails quickly by sending them to your personalized Evernote email as we discussed earlier in this book. Once your emails are moved, you can then go into Evernote and make sure that they have the right tags and are put into the proper notebook.

The reason that GTD and *The Secret Weapon Manifesto* work so well with Evernote resides in the power of Evernote itself. As you've learned from experience or from this book, Evernote is all about getting organized and being able to complete your tasks. GTD advocates getting any and all tasks out of your head and into a system. Evernote is that system. Then, *The Secret Weapon Manifesto* is injected and gives you a great way to organize and tag your tasks. If you use your email as a to-do list dumping ground, then you can utilize the Evernote personalized email address in order to quickly add your items to Evernote.